Unfurled

Nature Poetry

Penny Reilly

©2016

ISBN 978-0-9924759-7-0

Unfurled

Copyright © 2016 Penny Reilly

All rights reserved. No part of this book may be reproduced or transmitted in any form or by any means without written permission from the author, including electronic devices.

Photos Penny Reilly

Verse and Text Penny Reilly

Printed in Australia

Acknowledgement

Thank you Mother Earth for your inspiration!

Dedication...

To all who walk the greening way
Along the crooked path
into a new day
Where the air is clean
There is food for all
…nature unfurled, holds us in her thrall

…and to those readers who requested it. Enjoy!

Introduction

I am a Druid, a Bard. I am linked to the cycles and rhythms of nature as deeply as an in breath fills my lungs and as instinctively as a creature of the wild. When I look at the world and all her beauty, I cannot forget the simple principal of gratitude. My work is about honouring my place in the universe and to encourage others to do same.

Unfurled is a compilation of poems, some of which my readers will be familiar with, and many new.

My theme is the *unfurling* of things in their natural order, cycle and life expectancy, both physical and unseen.

This volume can be read in page sequence of seasonal change or just dipped into on a whim. Indeed, some of the verse is whimsical, while others take a darker path into the potential undoing of the very planet that sustains and gives us life.

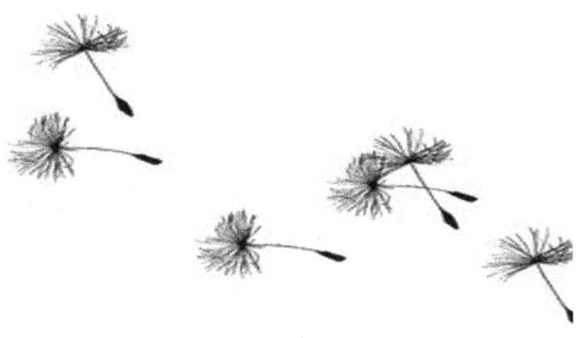

Autumn

Dance

Autumn Dance

Autumn encompasses three festivals in the Druid calendar. Lughnasadh, (Lugh's light), also known as Lammas (Loaf mass) is the first. Mabon; Autumn Equinox, when day and night reach equal lengths before tipping slowly toward Samhain (Sowen), (All Hallows Eve), known familiarly as Halloween and the beginning of Winter.

Lughnasadh is the time of the grain harvest and so the Wheel turns again toward Autumn. In the fields the bales are appearing as the farmer's work their way around the district, slashing, raking and baling their grain crop. Wheat is heading and the green crops of barley, rye and oats are ripening, shaking their pretty heads in the breeze.

It is the time of year Pagans make a sacrifice of something no longer needed. All outworn things must be let go, just as in the mythos the Lord of the Grain; John Barleycorn; The Greenman or Jack in the Green, to name a few, gives himself to the scythe of the farmer, that human kind can eat of his body, given willingly to the harvest.

This is the story of animated nature and the way of the Greenman who, by autumn, is a mature individual, if anthropomorphised as we are wont to do.

As much as he gives himself in sacrifice, so do we sacrifice something to give back into our community; our family by blood and by choice. Our code is to give willingly, with no thought of receipt.

In days gone by and in some small settlements all over the world today, the last grains harvested would be those used to bake the Lammas Bread to share and recognise the sacrifice and to inwardly digest the gift of life. The last stook or grain would then be made into a 'dolly' to place above the hearth for the season to protect from harm and bring prosperity to the home.

Of course some of this seed would be stored for the next planting cycle. This rite at Lughnasadh is a poignant and beautiful thing to see. In the worship of nature's animation, he becomes that last *stook* from which the doll is made to hang above the hearth. He is then free to walk the between, caring for animals and ensuring their safety for the coming cold months.

West is the direction in the southern hemisphere that we turn to as days draw in …water is the element of the West as we also look to the darker days ahead; a time to go within ourselves to reflect in our own emotional pools and tidal eddies.

Energy is the neutral force that binds and inhabits all things to the cycles of life, death and rebirth and then, once again the wheel spins on and Autumn deepens to Equinox, Mabon, when the lengths of day and night are equal. It is harvest time for apples and pears in cooler regions and soon olives too.

A season when nature is at her peak and we reap the rewards for our labours of sowing and growing. The sunlight diminishes and becomes more mellow; daylight hours shorten and dark hours extend. Here in southern hemisphere we can still have a beautiful *Indian Summer* ahead.

Crisp, cool starlit nights; the first frosts of the season make themselves felt and howling March gales with the accompanying storms begin to make it harder to work outside for long hours. By the time Samhain, known as Halloween to most, comes around the air is distinctly chill and the days are shortening. There is a feeling of gathering in. It's the last harvest of root vegetables and those such as pumpkin, squash and gourd.

For Pagans this is Celtic New Year …food is harvested …seeds have fallen and lay fallow; dormant for the gathering cold. I won't give credence here to what became of the ancient Samhain Rites, for they had nothing to do with Trick or Treat, or precocious children dressed as comic dwarves and ghouls.

It was the night when the Celts celebrated and welcomed their dead through ancestral lines. *A Dumb Feast,* (the table, laid as if for a feast with places set for the departed; their chair drawn back in welcome). There are many variations on this Rite but the translation is All Hallows Eve. Bale fires were lit on high hills and on village greens before the feast. After which, the ancestral presence returned to the Summerland. People would lock up their houses and burn little lights in carved, grimacing, pumpkin heads to ward of the spirits not invited to the feast, those of ill intent who had lost their way. Folk would remain indoors until midnight, the turning of the year. A dark haired man, carrying a piece of smoldering charcoal, would knock on the door. Embers were brought from the Bale Fires to light each hearth fire in a symbolic protection of house and village because for two more nights the veil between the realms of men and the lands of the otherworld remained thin and spirits allowed to roam at will.

In the mythos the Lady of Light and Shadows leads those led astray into a forest glade where the Horned Lord gathers them and leads them into the lands of the dead, where he remains until the Sun returns and she becomes a part of the sleeping earth again. As much as Autumn is a time of harvest and gain, so too is it a time of deep sleep and a sense of feeling on the edge of something approaching.

Quiet Approach

Autumn came on quiet feet
the earth, rising up to meet
...was showered with leaves of gold

A mist of many coloured hue
covering the earth in fragrant dew
...was showered with leaves of gold

A scent of filtered sunlight fled
over the earth, to become her bed
...was showered with leaves of gold...

Circle Dance

She changes her gown as the year grows old
from russet to amber, green to gold
She's the lady of the harvest for all living things
In the hedgerows and forests a rich bounty
She brings
He changes His cloak as She changes Her gown
They dance at Lammas' hay wain
'til in sacrifice, He's cut down
Yet they dance on and on
as the falling leaves twirl
Through the mossy glades twilight
to the pipes sobbing skirl
that breaks through the silence of a darkening year
Then on toward Mabon, the crisp air becomes clear
On they dance toward Samhain the ancestors awake
and the Wild Hunt comes riding the years'
fallen to take
Through the veil brightly gleaming
long hair darkly streaming
…and the hound's wild belling
cause the forests to shake

On; on yet they dance to Yule's last long dark day
the light becomes stronger
yet Jack Frost's still at play
but on they dance toward Imbolc
as the first lambs are born
Ever onward to bright Ostara
the sun's rays become warm
Then when May blossoms open
their honey perfumes the air
Step abroad as the sun rises
to make a wreath for your hair
For here at the rite of Beltane
their dance flames with bright joy
and folk may later harvest a girl or a boy
On to Litha they dance
sweet berries flavour the wine
the sun's power reaches zenith
and will slowly decline
On the breeze, you'll hear Her singing
In the thunder His rumbling mirth
When they call we'll dance with them
In circle spinning ...death to rebirth

Unfurled

Leaves stir; a gentle wind blows after the storm
Rippling still waters across the ponds
Nothing fits the pattern of the once-time norm
Reeds rustle; bracken unfurls green fronds
Blackbird sings
His cry of triumph rings
Autumn-flavoured colours, float and spin
Summer's last days, reflect gold on my skin

The Wild Hunt

The wild folk ride through forests green
Once a year they're easily seen
They come from beyond, the In-between
breaking through the veil
Their horns sound bright, voices light
Riding through the dark of night
faces oh so pale
The Wild Hunt rides, hounds at their sides
to chase the dark away
The Green Lord comes a'gathering in
all who were led astray
The Lady waits for them, in a lightened glen
where the Fae Folk play
He leads them on, through the forests fair
…to the Summerland far away.

Ebb and Flow

Her heart is silent Her, wings are frail
She heals suffering and in turn will ail
But she will find the way
to the edge of time
Hearing the night calls
following the rhyme
And the rhythm of life as it ebbs and flows
To the circle of stones
where the Magick knows
All the answers hidden, deep in her soul
She will find her way
to the edge of time
Where the Crooked Path
leads her to her goal

Ripening

She's changing her gown from green to gold
the harvest is ripening as the year grows old
Lughnasadh's first kiss is felt in the air
as elders ripen in hedgerows fair
What do you wish for your harvest this year?
Have you laboured long for your fruits to appear
Let go the old growth, let the leaves fall
The fruits of you harvest
will come when you call

A Lammas Tale

Daylight is fading
Winter draws in
Cold winds are blowing
ice on your skin.
Slowly as leaves fall
golden light fades
Dreams of snow falling
in quiet loamy glades
Weaving the magic in silent moonlight
Softly He comes in the frost
at dawn's light
A blanket of cover
Sparks on the earth
Listen carefully, you'll hear
…His deep bellied mirth

Lughnasadh Moon

A Lughnasadh moon smiles
in a darkening sky
She chases wild spirits
as the wind blows them by
A remnant of new
An instant of light
One moment of stillness
in the gathering night
A new cycle begins
new ideas taking shape
She smiles on your ventures
From her fragile moon scape
Sobs and laughter, joy and tea
The wheel turns on
through the spinning year
Celebrate the seasons
each in their own way
Dance the dance of life
Live in the moment every day

Depths

Watery depths of oceans and lake
calls your innermost soul to awake
Float in Her darkness, both salty and sweet
Ride Her waves to the shores of deep sleep
Life is Her gift, through the blood in your veins
Lymph fluid flows gently to pool and drain
through every cell and under your skin
Swim in Her depths ...find your tail, grow a fin
In Her darkest pools find your watery kin

Seasons Change

As the seasons change and the year moves on
listen closely, in the forest there's a wistful song
Though it's fading now as the windswept skies
blow a covering of leaves over where she lies
to sleep away the chilly hours
in woodland glade and dappled bowers
Small creatures flock to see her there
tying feathers and flowers in her fading hair
To watch her sleep and wait for spring
once again to hear her sing

Hollow Hills

A light, shines within hollow hills
if you may believe the truth
An entry to the realms of the Fae, I'm told
but none have returned with proof
For wander you might on a moonless night
And never again find the way
As madness creeps; into human blood seeps
Until insanity remembers the day
When in innocence you found your way underground
And in light and shadows played
Then in joy and desire you toyed with fire
You were enticed; you dallied then stayed
Is destiny then the ruler of men
or do we have our own voice
When darkness invades and daylight fades
do we indeed have a choice
Or is conscience the leveler that orders the way
…and our darkest dreams lead us back into day

My Song

My song
A whispering noted
mixed with joy and sorrow
Fear of change
lessens joy for the coming morrow
But when we cling
to life or any other thing
We only bring
the moment of its ending closer
My body
A vessel, created to hold my song
For right or wrong
we cannot judge its meaning
If we try
perhaps tomorrow die
within each note
there are my truths still gleaming

My notes

Which have bound me to my task

I ask

what point, the searching

Each word

each breath vibrates the web

…to encrypt my soul's bright urging

Body, mind and Spirit

A tapestry of life

spun off in rhythmic song

A chord

A crystal note

I'm bound to sing

No note sounds wrong

I vibrate

in colours; sounds

a rhythm growing

When sung

each note is spun

To shine

To awaken

…my deepest knowing

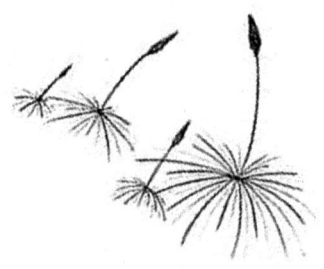

Shadows and Light

I dreamed of a creature with moon- shadowed eyes
Her hair all a'tangle. A Fae in disguise
She smiled at me fiercely, revealing white teeth
then opening her wings, flew away o'er the heath
I awoke with a start, the sun in my face
What had I witnessed, I felt blessed with grace
The next night was the same, her eyes violet ...aflame
She tugged at my sleeve whispered my name
When I awoke up the sunlight was gone
All that was left was a soft, fragile song
I pondered and wondered
who the creature might be
the reply came quickly
"Why I'm you and you're me"
So I dreamed of a creature; a Fae in disguise
and I gazed in the mirror
…at my moon-shadowed eyes

Dark Moon

Dark of moon the air is waiting
held in stasis for a call
Moonlit nights there's sound vibrating
holding us within Her thrall
Planets and stars in whirling orbits
dance the music of the spheres
Sweet, incandescent illuminations
far beyond our mortal ears
If these sounds, on occasion
came but once within our range
All our searching would be over
we would be forever changed

Yet the sweetness of this music
we can never understand
Never put with pen to paper
never play with human hand
For within are all the secrets
of every living universe
And in that changing we may wonder
is this a blessing or a curse
Scanning the heavens, ever listening
ever waiting for that call
As the sounding of all ages
…holds us in Her blissful thrall

Emotion Motion

Poppies red, in constant motion
Nodding heads in quiet breeze
Nothing judged
there is no emotion
No joy, nor grief
No cold to freeze
Being is a simple pleasure
Living now is all there is
Be the poppy or the heather
You were simply born for this

Ebb & Flow

Moon tides turning, fires burning
Winds blow cold across the land
Inner dreams and visions glowing
bringing warmth to cold, cold hands
Winters darkness now approaches
…creeping closer on tiptoe
Go within to seek the silence
Move in the cycles
...ebb and flow

Gateway

She is heard in the sigh of the whispering trees
In the notes of the calling sent on a breeze
Deep within you can hear Her magickal song
Deep within through the doorway
there's no right nor wrong
If you're quiet ...truly listen
hear her notes swell and dip
Through the rush of the ocean
or the rain as it drips
from each branch that bends
with the weight of her rain
or the soft scent of evening
that dulls sharpened pain

Along the Crooked Pathway
turning left and then right
you will hear her softly singing
the moonrise at night
Deeper still and you'll hear Her
at the gateway in the West
to the land of all dreaming
to complete your life's quest
And then onward; listen, you'll find your own thread
in a single note that sparkles, removing the dread
For nothing is dying only reaching its peak
In the depths, in Her darkness
…are the symphonies you seek

Harvest Blessings

The Lady walks in quiet fields
and flower faces smile
Golden petals, fragrant leaves
mile upon mile
When flowers fade; seedpods burst
and the greening is all done
the Goddess of the Harvest
…will bring home every one
So to our Harvest Lord and Lady
we bring our thanks today
for all the fruits, the barley corn
and fragrant golden hay;
For tender grapes on twisted vine
for Elders dark and green;
For the gift of life, you give to us
all hidden and unseen.
For flowing waters salt and sweet
Cool breezes through our hair
For all our furred and feathered friends
…and the planet that we share

Dawn in the forest as Her Magick breaks free

Hear Her song on the wind

as She stirs an ancient tree

In the depths, in the darkness

where all light is dim

A faint glow can be seen, at the edge of sight

on the rim

In your heart you sense Her

she calls ...a soft refrain

In your belly you feel Her ...a flutter

pangs of sweet pain

As your feet take you walking

into the depths of Her soft loam

you'll lay beneath Her fragrant moss

...finding home

Last Dance

Dance the last dance of Dragonfly
on delicate wings in an azure blue sky
Soon the first mists and
frosts of the time
will cover our land in icy rime
She will sleep the long sleep in enchanted pools
Her wings folded tight as the
planet cools
And then in the spring her
offspring emerge
to fly trembling again
On the brink. On the verge
For nothing ever truly dies
...as we dance the last dance of Dragonfly

Transition

Where do we move between here and there?
What do we become in transition and where
a place within of meanderings sweet or sour
...and then in sleep is lost many an hour, yet
Summer wings enfold me and I fly
Soaring; shadow-less I soar
Winter wings enfold me and I die
'til summer's sweet renewal comes once more
Ancient sounds emerging make their mark
Winter keeps her own notes in the dark
Spring's light brings the soft and fragrant tunes
while autumn sounds her notes like silver moons
All the while I watch and wait for you
too sing your song in many-coloured hue
Each season turns anew upon the wheel
When will you wake
...and in that sweet transition truly feel?

Wylde Dreamer

Deep within the Wylde dreamer stirs
Awakening from slumber as change occurs
Be willing to sense how your own needs are met
Stay awake, be aware
lest your dreams you forget
You are the sleeper and you are the dream
One and the same
it's within to be seen
You have slept long enough
Wake up human kin
Awaken the Wylde dreamer
...let the Magicks begin

Just for fun!

Chasing leaves as they turn to gold
Loving life like a child as the year grows old
Never forgetting to dance in the rain
To chase a dragonfly, feeling free, unrestrained
Crunchy underfoot, all earth and wood
Remember that childhood's
…not about being 'good'

Be playful no matter your age.
Nurture your free inner Spirit.

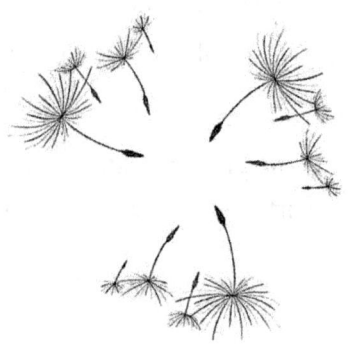

Winter

Dance

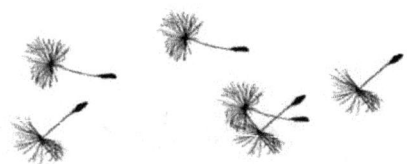

Winter Dance

History shows us that the earliest tribes of the planet understood the powers of life that lie in the darkness of the moon. In the three days when she is invisible to us and in the darkness reflected in a cold, misty Winter day, her affect is that of a transitional phase, between the death of the old and birth of the new. This dark time is a time of retreat, of healing and renewal, rather than one of fear; for dreaming of the future and the fallow times that come before outbursts of creativity and growth.

Samhain the start of Winter takes us into the transition. Our first Rite of the New Year post Samhain is then Yule. At Yule we reach the Winter Solstice and the days' tip again toward the light's return. Imbolc …named for the birthing time of lambs and the ewe milk gathered, gives us the first taste of Spring to come as some early fruiting trees begin to blossom and crocus show green tips above frosty ground. By the time we reach Ostara Spring returns and days are lengthening bright.

We all have dark phase times in our lives and they are naturally occurring periods in any life cycle. We often fail to understand that endings are the precursors to new beginnings; thus when our life rhythms move us into and through these dark phases, we can be ignorant of what is actually happening, (except of course with the benefit of hindsight) and that it is in actuality, a time of mystery, wisdom, and healing power.

There is less energy available for outdoor, 'doing' activities or for meeting the expectations of others, because the purpose of the dark phase and Winter time is to focus on the inner dimensions of our bodies and minds. If we can learn to attune ourselves to the natural rhythms of ebb and flow in our lives, we can use the intrinsic function of the dark times for this very healing and renewal. When we resist this inward motion in our psyche, then anxiety, stress, and fear are more likely to take hold of our emotions.

New things move beneath the surface of our psyche that will later rebirth into a new awareness; Magick is afoot.

Blue Moon at Samhain

Last night, Lady Moon was an eye in the sky
watching wild spirits as the wind blew them by
Sensing the veils thin, trees wept their leaves
As Samhain approaches the Lady bequeaths
all life that is fading She will renew
In silvery droplets of morning fresh dew

Fading Light

Daylight is fading
Winter draws in
Cold winds are blowing
ice on your skin
Slowly as leaves fall
golden light fades
Dreams of snow falling
in quiet loamy glades
Weaving the magic
in silent moonlight
Softly He comes
in the frosts of dawns' light
A blanket of cover
Sparks on the earth
Listen carefully; you will hear
…His deep-bellied mirth

Equality

Life and death all equal, all one
In life there's many little deaths
that cannot be undone
When you fight, when you yield
When you find the ways of truth
There's always a part of you that queries
needing proof
So look around and you will find
it's all inside yet, not in your mind
Life is a cycle the seasons turn
From life to death and then rebirth
It's this knowledge that makes you yearn
What's between
What can I say
You'll find out the truth for yourself one day

At the Edge of Dawn

The ghost of autumn lingers on
A scratching of leaves
A whispered bird song
But she waits in the night
Breathe her scent, feel her might,
in the lightning storm
at the cold edge of dawn,
In the rumbling thunder
Hold your breath don't go under;
For fear's not the way
it will flee before day
Winter's here; so is She
where the frost-giants play.

Falling into Dreams

Feel Her light on your skin
Draw Her in, draw Her in
Breathe Her into your core
deeper now than before
In your blood. through the lung
Her Magicks begun
Through your breath to your Heart
Through your brain
...feel it start
Be aware in the now
of Her Magickal light
Be still, breathe Her in. Listen
Watch Her Silver Orb glisten
She's still there on the
'dark of moon's' night...
Deep in the dreaming the
planet is waking
Oceans are rising the
earth realm is quaking
And yet. through all of the doomsayer fears
we may feel fearful, tender
...but we're STILL HERE!

Bones

We may be broken in our bones
In our heart
But life moves through us
if fragmented
Still we are not separate
never apart
Life drifts through all things
mending broken wings
Her call
heard in the night
through shadows and light
will catch us if we fall
like skeletal leaves
...in Her song

Aspects

When we speak of being ourselves
Winter aspects, hide away on shelves
Forgotten books
Deeper; looks
within
When 'I' speaks of 'me'
what does she see
Beyond agenda
Secret referenda
within
When 'me' speaks of 'I'
with a gentle sigh
of frustration
Asking for more animation
Causing agitation
within
I am the sum of many parts
Bleeding hearts
Forgotten arts
Dismissing my own desires
Smoldering fires
within

Delicate

She is small
Her wings are frail
Once brightest green
they're now so pale
She is so tired and needs to sleep
She'll bury down into the deep
How will she live
in all the smoke and dust,
the driving rains
earth's rumbling crust
Where will she go
fragile as snow
As you believe, so is she real
You may not see her
but you can feel
If you say no
she'll simply go
Just disappear
into the flow

Dance the Dance

A new moon smiles in a darkening sky

Chasing wild spirits as the wind blows them by

A remnant of new, an instant of light

A moment of stillness in the gathering night

A new cycle begins. New ideas taking shape

She smiles on your ventures

from her fragile moon scape

Sobs and laughter, joy and tears

the wheel turns on through the spinning year

Celebrate the seasons, each in their own way

Dance the dance of life

...live in the moment every day

Raven flight

Rustling feathers of
inky-black hue
Flying on wings
tipped with silvery dew
In the between through
the web she flew
Following the scent
as her time became due
The Mother was calling
and so she must fly
into the dark of a
moonless night sky
Soaring with joy
in the time she has left
Into the folds of the
warp and the weft

Winter Solstice

Yule is approaching
Hear the horns sound
Watch as Jack Frost
breathes ice on the ground
Coating the world in a silence of white
Sparkling like diamonds
on bright moonlit nights.
The Lady and Lord
come a gathering in
so make cauldron-brewed wassail
to share with your kin
Honey and nut cakes
for cold winter fare
to give the wee birds
to show them you care
Light up your candles
of red, green and white
...to act as a beacon of radiant light.

Yule

Water drips from ancient trees
Silent the birds
Still the bees
Rivulets of water
Currents run deep
Soon to wake earth
from a long winter's sleep
Gone longest night and the shortest of days
There's cold still to come
but Springs' on Her way
Not yet visible, not yet seen
but below the cold ground
the trees thoughts are of green
Slowly roots stirring it stretches to wake
Drinking in water
new buds to make
Ice and snow form
but in darkness below
New life awakens
…in beauty and flow.

Maelstrom

Whirlwinds, like talons barely sheathed
the gale howls in the night
In the dark the quiet disturbed by thunderous roll
flashing light
In deepest green, a sight unseen
by the folk who cower in their beds
Yet silver gleams as the moon beams
tear the dark to shreds
Calmer now the whirlwind spins a gentler tale to tell
but dangerous it seems; glass steams
for those who behind, misted windows dwell
Creatures stir ...silver wings whir
As nature decrees, trees weep their leaves
a whirling, spinning blur

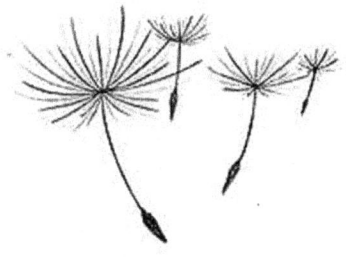

Spring

Dance

Spring Dance

Yule is followed by the Spring Rites of Imbolc (Ewes Milk), Beltane and Ostara, from which the word Easter came. Spring of course begins quietly, deep underground where the bulbs and tree roots shift and stir as a little warmth returns to the earth.

Everything about Spring Rites is about new life and fertility and yet in the early months, there are still the storms, rain and frost to contend with. Still, we begin to feel the change deep in the belly. For me it is as if I can feel the sap rising in the trees and my womb, though well past my own fertile days, quickens, as I sense the life stir beneath my feet.

A new cycle commences and the first flowers break ground. Blossoms begin to show bud and, by Beltane, the Hawthorn are alive with honey scented flowers; the bees make their first overtures in tentative appearances in the fresh morning sunshine.

Traditionally we make Hawthorn wreaths for our hair and of course dance the circle dance to invite fertility in, swathing a tree in bright ribbons of red, green and white. It's Hand-fasting time and couple jump the bonfire to make their vows for a year and a day. If they should conceive a child in that first year, they will remain together but if not they will have the choice to remain together or find a fertile partner. Nature is all about fecundity after all, particularly at this time of year.

Manifest Desire

It cannot be felt
Except deep in your core
It cannot be see
but you know there is more
And when it is seen
as the first shoots break ground
it happens in silence
No noise, not a sound
What you asked for at Mabon
will manifest the same
If not, simply wait
whisper Her name
It will come, as it must
in perfect love and perfect trust

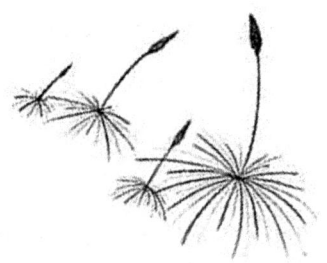

Invisible Emergence

Water drips from ancient trees
Silent the birds; still the bees
Rivulets of water; currents run deep
Soon to wake earth from Her long winters sleep
Gone longest night and the shortest of days
...there's cold still to come
but Springs on Her way
Not yet visible, not yet seen
but below the cold ground
the trees thoughts are of green
Slowly roots stirring She stretches to wake
drinking in water, new buds to make
Ice and snow form but in the darkness below
New life awakens in beauty and flow

Spring

She's stirring now
feel her push on your soul
Giving life, renewing, birthing
everything that's whole
Deep in the forests
He's running unseen
Soon they will wed
and give birth to the green

She's stirring now from amidst dead flowers
Quietly she slept
through the winter hours
Beneath the stretching
wild-wood bowers
Now spring returns
and the sweet rain showers
are washing away the dark

Deep Within the Greening

Within the greening, all is still
Waiting for a sense, a thrill
With goosebumps running
down your spine
you feel His presence
touch your mind
He's come to meet the Goddess fair
with flowers entwined
in Her wild-silk hair
He loves to catch you unaware
deep within the greening

Sisterhood

Walk with me sisters, though winds still blow chill
Take time to breathe, walk with me to the hill
Dance the serpent dance across sacred ground
See the sky changing; dawn breaks with no sound
In cold dark depths, spring awaits 'til
wildflowers unsheathe, to cover the hill
The moon and sun match their stride 'cross the sky
winter's cold grip breaks, once again the birds fly
A day filled with bird song
though mists wreath the grass
Their song breaks the silence as dancing we pass
With face lifted skyward
Our hearts filled with bliss
Soft dewfall brushes our hair like a kiss
Fragrant blossoms drip nectar
…bees busy in the sun
Walk, dance and fly with me sisters
summer has begun
Dance with me sister in the first summer dew
…open your arms …just a push
…SEE you flew!

Bright the Light

Bright the light that shines today
though the icy winds still blow
Bright the light that shines today
within the ebb and flow
For icy winds blow hope anew
Beneath the earth
Beneath cold dew
The bursting life once more renewed
By the Light that shines today

Wildlands

Heart of the wildlands
Spirits of old
What do you teach us
So gentle yet bold
Whom do you call on
as this new spring breaks.
Who will hear you
Who will awake
Will we stay sleeping
or will we wake up
to dance in your meadows
drink from your cup
Will we remember
as time's speeding by
Remember the greening
and fly

Singing Waters

Deep in the spring
where the waters sing
the source of all life
can be heard on the wing
You will hear Her song
once weak now strong
From the depth of the well
feel Her Magicks
Her spell
in liquid drops of first dew
as all life She renews

Dreaming Stars

Beyond the light
of dreaming stars
Beyond the light of time
I reached within to find a space
a place that's only mine
A place of light
and healing sounds
Yet darkness was its source
For from that darkness
light was born
and matter its resource

Grove

In a Grove of trees
there's a whispering breeze
that speaks of a land of wonder
When we hear the call
it soaks through to our soul
We float
We don't go under
When we listen with ease
Here that voice on the breeze
and we walk every day in the knowing
that the greening's begun
We don't walk ...we run
to the land of liquid light flowing
We are free in our hearts ...in our soul
All are one and in truth
all are whole

Release

Light streams
The Lady dreams
in silken showers of rain
Energy gleams
as the moon beams
Release to Her your pain
Rain showers
in once leafy bowers
where only bones remain
Cairns of stones
moss and bones
wild flowers blossom here
Spring will break
She will awake
returning life to the year
Swallows fly
in an endless sky
Release to Her your fear

Earth Mother Dreams

A windswept plain or a vast ocean deep
Are you awake or do you still sleep
As the needs of our world and its changing day
do you walk the pathway of the Greening Way
Warm winds blow as the spring air blooms
Fragrant blossoms scent the room
Wild ducks float on quiet ponds
under a canopy of willow wands
Swallows swoop in an endless sky
diving, catching small creatures that fly
on silvery wings over burgeoning trees
Catching the wind; sailing the breeze

Underneath all life a vibration plays out
When we truly hear; it dispels all doubt
Life is a challenge a dream; a gift
but we cannot afford to let our planet just drift
We can pretend it's alright
stick our head in the sand
Feel her heat like a furnace consuming the land
Scorching the grasses; burning the trees
until eventually we'll feel her ice on the breeze
Earth mother dreams but she's stirring now
again. if you listen she'll show you how
What are your tasks
What role will you play
...for the safe homecoming of the Greening Way

Souls and Soil

Trees …the mainstay of the earth
thrust their roots down deep
into the realm of loamy things
and little bugs that keep
the soil's sweet smell and fertile strength
that all things need to grow
and yet we let our soils (souls) deplete
earth's death is long and slow
So grow your garden well my friends
…it keeps your soil (soul) complete

Mists roll in ...the Magpies sing

their welcome to the morning

With throats arched high ...toward the sky

they sing their song of dawning

Of daybreak and a season new

When every grass blade ...graced with dew

bows to the sun's bright rays anew

...to welcome in the day

Stirring

She sees you, knows you
to the depth of your soul
She waits for you to remember
energies that make you whole
It's time, She speaks
to wake from sleep
Stir the powers slumbering deep
Call them in
call them home
from the mist where they roam
Emotions pool
Waters foam
Tidal flows become a flood
Awakening memory in your blood
Stir from sleep
from slumbers deep
It's time to know you're home

The Watcher

She watches with eyes that see through to your soul
She sends the music to heal; make you whole
Touching with a breath, warming and kind
To removing the veil that once kept you blind
to the innermost reaches of a mind filled with fear
refreshing your spirit
It all becomes clear
for you do have a purpose
it's simply to live
with joy and passion, to share and give
others encouragement
Those who are tortured and blind
Send them strength, send them hope …be kind

Spring's Herald

Spring's on the way.
Light the flame, light the flame
Dance in morning dew
Call Her name, call Her name
We are here, we can see you
We are the same, all the same
Bright dawns the day
Shining bright, shining bright
Thrush calls the morning
In the light, in the light
Gathering momentum
Equal day, equal night

Can you sense the sap rise
in the trees, in the trees
Smell the scented blossom
on the breeze, on the breeze
Sweet, wet soils fragrant as
I'm on my knees, on my knees
Spring's on the way
Play with us, light the flame
Sing with the Song Thrush
It's a game, all a game
Cycles within circles
Seasons change, spin on ...and on
Winter's light fades
Soon all shadows are gone

Entangled Weave

At times we walk a darker path
when threads entangled weave
A twisted path, a song-less way
breaking free of darkened days
that captivate to deceive
A lighter day dawns clear and bright
when threads unraveled weave
a Crooked pathway into day
where all may find reprieve
A journey in, the tapestry stretched
the shining veil wears thin
transparent is the way
through silvered threads that sway
to glowing, sun-drenched bowers within

Summer

Dance

Summer Dance

Another spin of the wheel and Summer comes around again. In the changing season between Spring and Summer the air is full of the cries of birds, fighting, squabbling over nesting sites, food and just because it's their nature.

By the time Summer Solstice comes around and the year begins the slide toward Lughnasadh again the bounty and beauty of nature are evident in every byway and hedgerow.

At Litha, Summer Solstice we are thankful when crops are abundant, fruit and vegetables vie for position in greenhouse and garden bed and there is nothing like the taste of a freshly harvested tomato with basil picked and eaten immediately.

The light begins to change; it's subtle at first but eventually as the season moves deeper toward Autumn, one again the elderberries ripen, blackberries are for the taking around the woodlands and hawthorn and rowan begin to take on the colours of Autumn's mantle again.

Beltane Prelude

Hear the winds calling
a sultry refrain
He's out and about
the prelude to Beltane
He can be heard
in the rustling of leaves
He sends small reminders
to tug at your sleeves

He Says...

I am the essence that lives
all unseen
I am the memory
of all that is green
Take up the mantle
of earth's greening time
Smell the wild's fragrance
like fresh summer wine
Come to your circle in
Hawthorn arrayed
I'll meet you in the Greenwood
where my music is made

He's returning now
from the woodland glade
From beneath the trees
of which he's made
Through winter he ran
and all debts he paid
for those who killed his kin
with the blade
Now the greening has begun

Spring's return has us all aglow
Water trickles
from the melting snow
Her flowering mantle
puts on a show
and the preening birds
with the rivers flow
Life returns to the land

Summer Lord

He walks the land again tall and strong
So many myths say he's evil and wrong
One look in His face, the warmth in His eyes will show you the truth of His ways
As He walks with the Lady, trust in that smile as He shows you the new greening days

Summer Heat

Sun-drenched garden
sleepy birds
Whispering something
I can almost hear the words
Muttered oaths from panting beaks
Catching drops from plants that leak
their gooey moisture
sap running free
I sit exhausted
beneath a friendly tree

Red Lady

Red lady rides at the edge of dawn
Cross winds blow fire to the waiting storm
Silence is cold as solar storms howl
broken only by mournful hoots of an owl
What lies waiting on the edge of time
Who can translate the red ladies rhyme
Fast moving comets predict the fall
as waking, sweat bathed
we hear her haunting call

Dance

Danced at dawn
as the earth was waking
Danced as the sun rose
A fiery ball
Danced as the earth slept
Danced as the winds rose
Danced 'til I found home
...in Oneness with All

Erupting

Erupting

Out of the dark

A power without sound

leaves its mark

…on unsuspecting minds

And yet, if we listen we may hear

A note

A sound beyond the range of mortal ear

…or human kind

Eruption

From the depths of earth

A sound that freezes skin

…denying mirth

Trembling all that lives

As nature takes

…and gives

Warmth, spreads, fire heats
Rebirth
With open eyes
A force beyond the skies
Trembling hands
To equal shattered lands
As widening bands
…of knowledge spread
Or is that only in our head
those memories of ancestry
…our kin
Erupting truth
Forever seeking proof
When conscious knowing dies
A force beyond the skies
…still lives
…within

Dryads Summer Dance

Dryads dance their circle round
with eerie flight that makes no sound
Over mossy green and stony ground
be still …don't let yourself be found
For if they see you're wide eyed gaze
a glamour may fall
eyes droop as they glaze
over in wonder …it will amaze
as you circle with them in a feverous daze
They will sing and chant
A bell-like call
You will dance with them
'till to the ground you'll fall
On and on through the night
under a full moon's thrall
to wake stiff and spent in a sleepy sprawl

Sunset in vibrant colours Sunrise; liquid gold
Autumn light is dusty, fading
another year grows old
Grass besprent with rainbow dew drops
Tiny spiders weave and fly
On silver threads they hurtle skyward
Unafraid to live or die
Purple berries, umber clusters
Brambles full of berries, fat
Fox enjoys them (this is clear by
the dark blue, seed-filled scat)
Bees are busy, Kookaburras chuckle
sitting waiting for their meal
Nature blossoms, fruits and dies
I observe, my thoughts surreal

Values

Value the dark
as the equal of day
Value the night
when darkness holds sway
Value Summer sunlight
rich and warm on your skin
Find balance here
Your only enemy lives within

Sylph

The sylph of the tree
shook her flowers at me
and told me to play on the wind
She said I could ride
hold my arms out and glide
If I fell she'd be there to catch me
So we fly and we soar
though no one's keeping score
as we laugh at the world down below
But she's canny and wise
taking me by surprise
as she shows me the rivers that flow
They are filled with stuff
plastic garbage ...enough
to fill an ocean or two
So I say to you here
take a stand, make it clear
Stop it now, if you hold Her dear
It's all up to us
In Perfect Love and Perfect Trust

The Way

To know the Way is to know yourself
Be that your inner child or your inner elf
To walk the Way is to know the lands
To grow your food with your own two hands
To be a Wytch is a way of life
Keeping the truths in a world torn with strife
Being Her ears and eyes in the mists
Using your sight, sharing your gifts
Being gentle with self and with those who can't see
Don't give up on this world ...sisters and brothers
…there's still you ...and there's me

Honouring

On this day and in this hour
Dance in her honour
Feel your own power
Bathe in her flame
For an hour or so
give up all your pain
Let Magick spark lightness
Build energy within
Then let fall all cares
Dance free in your skin
Let no one ever tell you
to enjoy life is a sin
Breathe deeply just let go
...breathe Her in

Wonder & Dream

Dare to wonder dare to dream
when moonlight pools and things unseen
move and fly on gossamer wing
as hidden Fae their anthems sing,
to Lord and Lady fair and bright
gathering souls to aid their flight
to places green where Magicks reign
where all are healed of fear and pain...

The Other

Can you see her, is she real
If you don't believe in her, her fate is sealed
In her eyes dark depths, a sadness unconcealed
"Remember me," she says,
"when my face to you I did reveal
You were a child and I your one true friend
When you were sick, I helped your body mend
When you were sad, I wiped your tears away
...and then as one
in the greenwood we would play
Where did you go
I've been waiting all along
If you wake up, remember me
it's been so long
I'm lonely here and miss your joy and fear
But if you don't come back
...into the green I'll simply, disappear."

Chalice

Drink from my cup and your soul is healed

Take of my breath and your life is sealed

Deep within as your memories awake

Fly swift to the greening

my healing waters to take

Come to my well, the font of all life

Clear now your minds and be free of strife

For the truth is within let go all the lies

Come dance in my meadows

…I will open your eyes

Ask

Within the cauldron of knowledge
is every answer you seek
Ask for aid, feel it bubbling
boiling over at its peak
Scry in Her pools, build the power,
let it simmer more and more
See the answers slowly forming,
vibrating deep into your core
the truth of all the ages is contained
within one tiny drop
and all the little drops together
equal that which never stops
never ending, constantly flowing
as your truth you find within
every lifetime, every person,
every tribe you've known as kin
as truth from the deep emerging,
gives you pause for silent thought
take a breath, look deeper still
for here is everything you sought

Hear Her Song

She floats on the day
The trees bow and sway
Never broken for long
She can heal with her song
Listen now hear her call
She'll not let you fall
Take her hand let her lead
She has all that you need
You'll not be broken for long
She will heal with her song
Just let go and she's there
Tender hands stroke your hair
When you're sad just give in
Feeling frail's no sin
There's no need to be strong
Just listen ...be still
...hear her song

Jump the Pyre

Dance of fire
Jump the pyre
Revel with the lady of the flame
Dance through the night
Feel your power with delight
Free yourself ...give away pain
Nothing to lose; much to gain
Fire cleanses; heals
Wounds renew, old skin peels
Waking warmth as it grows within
Summer abundance, births new green
Blossoms fragrant fall to fruit now seen
Jump the pyre; revel
...in the warmth on your skin.

Moontides

Moontides turn and sunlight fades
Shadows lengthen in dappled glades
Rain showers fall in bright cascades
...another season's done
Fast falling dark in midnight blues
Forsaken all the coloured hues
Grasses now bedecked with dew
...another season's done
Frost and ice the grasses cover
All warmth gone
All brightness smothered
Misty morning
Blackbird's warning
...another season's done

Feel her cold breath

Winter draws in

Icy winds blow

the lake freezes thin

Layers of stories lost in the Mists

Places of mystery

Magickal gifts

Standing stones rooted

Sentinels to loss

What words do they whisper

What's hid 'neath their moss

Dance the In-between

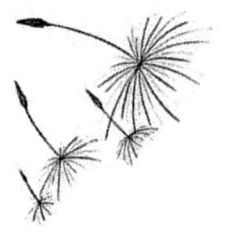

Dance the Dance of Life

In-Between

We dance the dance as seasons Unfurled and in part perhaps, many of us separate ourselves, from what is the very thing that gives us life and reason.

We shed skin follicles, hair, droplets of fluid from sweat, tears, spittle etc., not to mention other bodily functions, solids, and fluids. These particles that bear our 'Siegel', our unique signature of who we are, are constantly and eternally drifting out into the universe to share themselves, (which explains themselves), to anything else they come into contact with that resonates with something we may align with, learn from or simply merge with. I am sure you've all heard the phrase 'we are made of the stuff of the stars,' …well of course we are!

A tree in the forest communicates with everything around it in the same manner in order for creatures to understand its signature as 'eat me' or 'eat me at your peril'. It's only humans, stupid enough to forget the signatures of the forests; forget the signatures of the elements in weather behaviour etc.!

The communication of that same tree is no different to our Siegel of skin, hair spittle etc., it loses leaves, seed pods and seed go into the ground to grow; dust from its bark and the bark itself falls and become particles that fly off to join with others to create something else. Eventually the whole tree will rot and fall, does it question that? It's really only us that say 'oh no you can't dispose of my body like that you can't let it rot where it is like all the other creatures of the forest! Yes, ceremony for our dead is important but how the body disperses into those particles in the Dance of Life is probably the moot point… and that is our reaction versus response that has made us the way we are around life and death itself.

How long nature will tolerate our stupidity is another matter entirely. Resources, food, water and the eternal need for man to wage war will be the deciding factor in the next few years. Mother Earth is infinite in herself but she will alter and change to fit a new mold of her own making. It remains to be seen if we can fit her mold, follow her ways or whether we will go the way of any transient being that walks her lands, into extinction.

There is a moment. I call it the Quickening a moment that bridges the seasons, when something in between is on the edge …the verge of change and transformation.

Are You In

If a dream you had
to change your world
Where would you begin
To be yourself or someone else
To be more like your kin
If you're wanting other "parts"
to manifest within
If I were to knock upon your door
...would there be anyone in

Warning

A warning is sent to those who believe
their Magicks are so strong
Forgetting the law of 'harm ye none'
Beware lest you are wrong
Magick unsanctioned is a tool of dissent
and like all dissention returns
directly to the one who sent
For those who believe that it's okay
to wield such negative power
through ill intention
watch out …for your Magick will turn sour
It's not for the Wytch to send others their will
Belief is one thing but the truth remains …still
that all Magick is wrought with a deep love of life
Beware for the Lady is watching
when using power to bring strife
For strife it will be awaiting those
who abuse the Mother's Way
…and in some form …unexpectedly
…will return to the wielder one day

Make it You

Night drifts into day there's so much in play
as the planet spins on through space
We take it as given it will always be here
but have you truly found your place
As the stars spin away and night drifts into day
can you say you have done all you can
Is the world better for you
Have you lived life with grace
or do you sense this is the downfall of man
Have we all done our best
Have we worked without rest
to fulfil the dreams of a greening life
When we came here to play
did we dream of this day
as the planet is torn by war and strife
So if you feel there's more to do
don't speak of 'they', rather make it 'you'
who travels the earth path with joy, not fear
Then who knows, if we're strong
we may right the wrong
…to renew the world and dry each child's tear

Frost on the Moon

Cold seeps as the moon creeps
throwing light in the room
Frost crisps as the mist wisps
float gently in the gloom
Day breaks as the sun wakes
song fills the air
Dawn's light, slowly growing bright
joy felt, no despair
Only relief felt ...as in mulch I knelt
to harvest the old
As the year dies, how time flies
...as leaves turn to gold

Lives Within Lives

Lives within lives
Many doorways of the soul
Even those in disguise lead you home
make you whole
We are not always kind
when we're troubled of mind
but in truth it's a game
we're all one all the same
Lives within lives
Many twists and turns in time
Through the mists, lost in the rhyme
Yet the way becomes clear
when we follow what's most dear
In our belly, in our heart
...not separate, nor yet apart

Eyes

Eyes the window to the soul
Look within to see the whole
...of the inner heart and busy mind
Leave the ego self behind
Deeper still to the world inside
Where are you there ...or do you hide
from other's stares or a wayward glance
Straightening shoulders ...taking a stance
Do you trust who lives in there
Let them out ...show yourself
Do you dare

Turning Left

There's a doorway that takes us to a timeless space
where all that we dream may be found in one place
Offering ourselves to the pathways between
brings truth to our journey
...to where we've already been
We can never go back, only here in the now
do we remember the times
when we made a sacred vow
To walk the Crooked Pathway
turning left and then right
Beyond pain and pleasure, beyond the fear of night
We walk out of the darkness
…into the warmth of Her light

Burrow Deep

Worlds between worlds
Lives within lives
Fly swift as a bird
Be a fish as it dives
Smell the soil
Burrow deep
Feel the earth
Does she sleep
Nestle in worming down
Be a bug in the ground
Be a cell in its skin
Go between
Go within
In all that space
Is all we are
Will be
And
Have ever been

Call to Her

She walks the path of the ancient of days
as they twist and turn on the Crooked Path's way
Through the trees of the forest
whose powers once held sway
Now diminished in the mists far away
Call to her ...bring her back
Feel the pain; feel the lack
Feel the sorrow of so many who grieve
Call her back
Quickly now
...before she leaves

The Crooked Path

As the Crooked Path wanders

through the back roads of time

hear a sound; a whisper ...a song ...a rhyme

As the pathway; enchanted; moves left and then right

through the sun-streaming morning

to the star-shine of night

Listen to the rhythm of the song that you hear

It's for you and you only

Your song for a changing year...

I'll Disappear

Can you see her, is she real?
If you don't believe in her, her fate is sealed
In her eyes dark depths, a sadness unconcealed
Remember me, she says
...when my face to you I did reveal
You were a child and I your one true friend
When you were sick, I helped your body mend
When you were sad, I wiped your tears away
...and then as one, in the greenwood we would play
Where did you go?
I've been waiting; did I do wrong?
If you wake up, remember me ...it's been so long
I'm lonely here and miss your joy and fear
...but if you don't come back
...into the green I'll disappear

Take Flight

Follow the pathway of your dreams
Create the scenarios in your mind
What thoughts inhibit your success
What happens in the process to make you blind
...to the fact that success is yours within
In your head, your heart
it's under your skin
Be aware ...dare to dream
as the calling is heard
Take a chance ...spreads your wings
Take flight
...be as free as a bird

Frailty

For those who are frail and cannot speak
and to those who are not heard
...their voices weak
To all who mourn for what can never be
give them your heart
...give them your energy
We may make choices ...even when we're strong
that later manifest ...twisted
...somehow wrong
Send them your love, without the need for show
With compassionate strength
send love over conflict
...let them go...

Cherish

Cherish each other
Love one another
…the law is "harm ye none!"
Gift to each other the truth of yourself …and earth's greening will be done.
Find you the innocence of gentler days Come to the forests where Faefolk play
Live in the moment as if t'were your last day
…and earth's greening will be done

Layers

Layers of awareness are awakened by our dreams
Our consciousness is hindered
…by the "doing," plans and schemes
If we could simply let the "now,"
…become our journey's theme
Then we would soon discover
…not the "how"
…but what living truly means

What the Cost?

We are forever seeking home
throughout the stars
the universe we roam
and though our mortal souls are never lost
...our humanness will ever pay the cost
Look deep within the wounded bleeding heart
...what challenge lies ...believing we're apart
Separation, loneliness and tears
...and yet we are not homeless as we fear
Our body, mind and spirit are the same
the sense of homelessness is but a mortal game
In order that we search and finally find
and even that is found
...within the labyrinth of our mind

The Seer's Isles

The Seer's Isle
the isle of dreams
hidden beyond the Mists of Time
Beyond the lands of human schemes
...a land of great design

For deep within, the Magicks return
If you feel your heart race it's for this that it yearns
So wake up human child and before the year turns
Feel the fire in your belly
...let it burn

A coracle drifts across waters deep
to the Seer's Isle the land within sleep
where the Otter swims free
on the shore stands the Deer
...and the Raven flies beyond all mortal fear

Avalon of the Heart in the swirling Mist
Moist drops on your skin, as soft as a kiss
Where the song of all Time is heard in the deep
...and the Mother calls to you in your sleep

Wake up human child come dance with the wind
Wake up and see where new life can begin
Feel the sun on your face and the breeze in your hair
...wake up human child, let go mortal care

For the world is renewing
If you wait it will cease
You will miss the Quickening
of the Green Ways of peace
She has waited so long for you all to awake
So wake up human child
...for your own sweet sake...

Cerridwen

Energies deepen
Time to go in
Deep into the heart
where all things begin
She watches and waits
Stirs the cauldron of life
Keeping you, safe
from all trouble
...all strife.
When you love, when you trust
When you live "now" not "when"
journey inward
She'll be there
...Cerridwen

Prophecy

A shuddering breath
A belaboured cry
A ragged gaze from blind, unblinking eye
For all her wisdom; knowing she must die
Seeing; a gift too much to bear
A prophecy, in the light of day
too burdensome to share
For, "Know Thyself" the motto emblazoned there
Fate riddled; she alone shall care
In darkness, where all prophecy grows
Becoming real, as light upon it shows
…that all are fated in the blood that flows
While the heartbeat of the world; daunted slows
Tainted elixir; passed in sips
Her mouth dry, it burns upon her lips
A prophecy of death, as pale hand slips
and shattered, falling
…tastes only sweet rosehips

Saga of Perfect Love

Perfect Love and perfect trust
is all that we should know;
To rise above life's cut and thrust
we have a way to go
The darkness birthed within each soul
it's offspring, known as fear
and in that fearing we forgot
the love that brought us here.
A greening globe, a shining sphere
that once knew only light,
Was spun from orbit, falling deep
into the realms of night
Once we knew the silken threads
that held us strong and tight
Not to bind us but to stretch
to help our soul's winged flight
That guiding reign of pure intent
forgotten in the deep, is now ascending
...pulling to awaken us from sleep.

The web of light around this orb
our home away from home
Birthed simply for Her Light to feel
the darkness of alone
So now we feel Her driving force as She reels us in
And one by one we must ascend
re-joining with our kin.
It's not that we must leave this realm
the reverse in fact is true
for there are also other kin who left our Planet Blue.
They were the Fae, the conquered race
who could not stand the dark
Who then withdrew and human kind
were left to make their mark
But what a legacy we leave
now that we're almost done
and who in truth remembers the one law
…"with harm to none."

No guilt, no fears, no human tears
can heal the rift we wrought,
And if that's so, has our descent
been truly, all for naught.
The Mother knows, She hold the threads
She guides us even here,
to the depths of life's illusive paths
each step a mortal year.
Each birth anew upon the Wheel
together yet apart,
We now as one ascend to heal
Earth's frail and failing heart.
We feel the pull, as thinning veils
let us see beyond
as the Fae return, bringing light
…once hidden …almost gone.

This realm of beauty and of love
cannot be as before
This turning sphere of spinning threads
must change to be restored.
So once again as life ascends
and dark is filled with light
we see all that is mirrored
as once day gave way to night.
No separation truly is, between each soul each spark
and She has never truly let us fall into the dark
For half of Her is Light indeed
as Her other is the Night
and our descent was that we learn
we're always in Her sight.
Never alone, never lost, never left to die,
She shone within us all along
She taught us how to fly.
In freedom, joy and clear intent
we fly the well of fears
Once more renewed, reclaimed, rebirthed
.... we're cleansed by mortal tears

Cairn of Bones

In a circle of stones …lies a cairn of bones
that tells of an age long gone by
In a grove of trees …a song of ease
whispers a fragrant lullaby
All is found within …all the lore, all your kin
who have ever trodden the land
Find their true nature here in each passing year
the gifts that you hold in your hand
In each cell you relate to the Druid Bard or Ovate
who remember the message in the stones
and in the song of the trees
whispered low on the breeze
simply listen to find your way home

Changed, Never Dead

Don't enter the woods with a blade
don't taint the sacred glade
Be aware of the iron that injures the Fae
driving them forever through the veil; away
Be gentle with creatures you don't understand
Take time to learn …listen to the land
We are not the only beings here
leave your blade at home …no need to fear
for if your heart holds courage
is gentle yet bold
they will appear to you
…all the creatures of old
Or she will lie down to sleep again
to leave this place …the land of men
to join with the wildlings
…to play in the fields
As autumn approaches and the grain harvest yields
abundance and plenty to make Lammas Bread
She is joined by the Hunter
who is changed …never dead

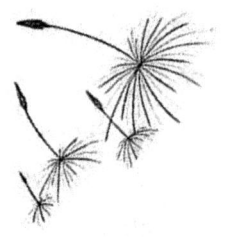

Raven flight

Rustling feathers of inky-black hue
Flying on wings tipped with silvery dew
In between time through the veil she flew
Following the scent as her time became due
For the Mother is calling and soon she must fly
Into the dark of a moonless night sky
Soaring with joy in the time she has left
...into the folds of the warp and the weft

Circle of One

Build your circle of one
Healing Magick's begun
You're never alone
There's every tree, every stone...
waiting, listening to your dreams in the night
Cast your circle of one
let your Magicks take flight...
With every breath that you take
every whisper, every song
put your trust in Wylde nature
you can never go wrong
Stand in circle call them in
ask for aid from your Fae kin
Cast your circle of one
...healing Magick's begun

Men-an-Tol

Step through the veil to the lands of the Fae

Step from starlight into bright day

A mystical dance will unfold as you stray

...through the Men-an-Tol, where the Wildlings play

Lake of the Moon

A pathway opened to the lake of the moon
Her light cast a spell dismissing the gloom
Shadows reflecting on the wall of my room
sent a frisson of energy into my broom
Come fly with me lady
said the moon's shadow self
Come join with your siblings, the Fae and the elf
Bring your wings if wish and a robe for the night
Come play with me sister
Moon bathe in my light

Release

Light streams

the Lady dreams

...in silken showers of rain

Energy gleams

as the moon beams

...release to Her your pain

Rain showers

in once leafy bowers

...where only bones remain

Cairns of stones

moss and bones

...wild flowers blossom here

Spring will break

She will awake

...returning life to the year

Swallows fly

endless sky

...release to Her your fear

Fox-changer

I'm not all I seem
Let me into your dream
and I'll show you the ways between time
But to follow me there first, come to my lair
Trust me to answer a rhyme
Ask me all you will, I have consummate skill
to travel all threads of Her song
Remember in truth it is all by your will
you learn which tone's right or sings wrong
As the way becomes thin
come follow your kin
as they tread the roadways between
For you're not all you seem
and if you enter my dream
I'll teach you to shape change your skin

Trueshapes

As we believe, so it is true
Even shape is illusion knowledge hidden in you
When you remember, when you awake
Who will you be, what is your true shape
Raven or owl ...fox or blue jay
Each is within, find the key there today
When you remember, when you awake
Who are you really, what is your true shape
In every cell of your being a memory lies
It's not found in the ethers, nor in deep blue skies
When you remember, when you awake
Who are you truly, what form will you take?
There are choices we make to create our form
when the truth becomes manifest
we are more than 'onceborn'
When you remember, when you wake up
you can sip from Her cauldron
...drink deep from Her cup

Shape changer

Shifting, changing
Morphing, rearranging
Bones creaking, skin sliding
Stretching, wings widening
Soaring, song outpouring
Drifting, weight shifting
Light gleaming
Feathers streaming
Eyes glistening, deepest listening
Body tightens; senses heighten
Turns, spinning, dives, winning
Beak snatching, talons catching
Load bearing, flesh tearing,
Hunger sated, warm, elated
Strength fed, soon feathers shed
Re shaping, almost breaking
Freedom waning
Shifting, changing
Morphing, rearranging

Owl Wind

Winds howl and the cries of the owl
are heard in the dark all around
Air shrieks as the ice creaks
the frost breathes white on the ground
Wintry night, rabbit screams in fright
at the night jars cry on the gale
Trees moan, branches shake and groan
at the roaring, ice filled hale
Moon rise, though the darkened skies
are full of shifting cloud
Still she walks, back straight, she stalks
head high, aloof and proud
.Lady Arianrhod brings the night
Silver hair, streaked with light
Owl flies at Her side
When she calls to you, watch what you do
she will cleanse you of your pride
The Silver Wheel turns on and within Her song
you will hear the tune she brings
Listen now, be careful how
you interpret what she sings

Wyche Wheel

Eight the trees of Wyche ways known
and in between the five are sown
Eight the Sabbats round the wheel
Five the elements that harm or heal

Spirit the fifth that binds the five
...as the Wyche wheel spins all human lives

Earth the Spirit; physical Life and Death
Air the spirit that gives us breath
Water the Spirit; pooled emotions deep
Fire the Spirit that wakes us from sleep

Spirit the fifth that binds the five
...as the Wyche wheel spins all human lives

Around we spin and around again
Emotions rich; joy and pain
Spring, Summer Autumn, Winter chills
Dance the circle dance on the dreaming hills

Spirit the fifth that binds the five
...as the Wyche wheel spins all human lives

Rhythm

In the mists of time
where all made sense of the rhyme
there's a sound that streams
like endless dreams
passing in notes sublime
Who are the Fae who walk the Old Way
To where did they stray, when they left that day
You can hear them still
put your ear to the hill
you'll hear the wild music they play
Rhythms grow as the trees dance and blow
in an unseen wind off the heath
Drums rumble, summoning from beneath
The earth splits wide, pouring out the Fae ride
...their songs they do bequeath

Walk softly, they sing
Let joy your notes bring
to a world that is cold; a world grown old
Let go your fears ...treasure passing years
Let go; no need to cling
Joy will return; bellies fed
Passion burns
...as their music returns
Let your feet tap and glide
while their haunting notes slide
...fill to the brim, your soul that yearns

Into the Dreaming

Where do you go in your dreams
Are you sure you're awake
Do you follow your heart
or react for reacting's sake
Where are you when you are dreaming
Is it a peaceful place
Do you go to the lands of beauty
to a Sacred greening space
How do you feel in the morning
are you truly here
Or are you really still dreaming
'til small whispers of truth appear
Do you dream of a journey
Do you know where to
Is it long and exciting
in the dream are you ...you
Does it feel like a memory, written deep in your cells
An island of apples and a deep icy well
Who travels with you or are you alone
Do you feel lost
…or are you travelling home

Musings of a Story Teller

Candle light dream the owl flies unseen
She takes me to travel the threads
where a new story's born ...new pages adorn
the book as it flows from my head
As words tumble out ...I awake with a shout
What was that new thread I found?
but sometimes it's gone ...fleeting words in a song
and at others, recalled to be bound
in a journal of thoughts as a new tale is wrought
that continues to push at my soul
So settle I must and in my muse trust
...so the journey unfolds ...becomes whole

Oneness in Duality

Half-light – half dark
A dove's coo – a dog's bark
Half dark – half light
Her lantern still burns bright
Sunrise – sunset
Gleaming pearls – blackest jet
Sunset – sunrise
Scry in the deep pools
Craft of the Wise
As Above – So Below
Outer light – inner glow
As Without – So Within
All That Is
Mirrored in your kin
Half dark – half light
Raven calls the day
Owl hunts the night
Half-light – half dark
Foxes slinking – trilling lark
No division – under the sun
No separation – All is One

Can You Fly?

Can you fly?
No regrets and no goodbye
Can you simply spread your wings
...and fly
Can you dream
or does illusion bind your wings
As watery depths enfold you, coldness stings
...can you dream
Can you try
to break the shackles binding flight
When dreamless sleep's enfolding halts the fight
...can you try
Can you soar?
No fear of drowning
flying. Falling
as lights beyond beckon. Calling
...can you soar
Can you fly
No regrets and no goodbye
Can you simply spread your wings
…and fly

Wytch Way Round

Wyche way round does the Magick flow
does it ever stop,
Is it always on the move
…ever on the go
Wyche way round does the oak leaf know
when it's time to fall
From seed to shoot
how does it know
…it could ever grow so tall

Wyche way round does the caterpillar know

how to spin

to the left or to the right

…to cocoon itself in

Wyche way round does a butterfly know

when to first emerge

then wings open, drying

…trembles on the verge

Wyche way round does the dragonfly know
the exact time
to crawl from water onto earth
…before taking to the sky
Wyche way round does a honey bee know
it never needs to roam
yet flitting over vast expanses
…always finds home

The Book of Life

If you could live inside a book
the one you read in a quiet nook,
where would it take you, how would it look
Would it be sumptuous, a travelling feast
Would it have dragons and other such beasts.
Would it be sad or a place of content
Would it be in a castle or in a red tent
Who would you be in the pages you read
A saint or an angel; a vampire that feeds
What would you look like, would you be fair
Would you have ringlets; long tresses of hair
Would you have friend or be alone
Would you be happy or constantly moan
Who would you be in the pages within
Whoever you are enjoy the journey
she said with a grin

The Youngest Child

I am made of many coloured threads
that twist their way between joy and dread
I would rather be alive than dead
…I am the youngest child

I am supple of both body and mind
I always fought the way of daily grind
I shout to the world, "Wake up, are you all blind"
…frustrated as the youngest child

I would run wild, free in spirit through the trees
I could fly …I always hid my bleeding knees
For sadness comes, when even the friendliest breeze
…inhibits the youngest child

Now there are but two of us, one sibling gone
the middle child, petitioner against all wrong
In the sibling world, the eldest ruled, was strong
We do not speak often, for I
no weakling, am the youngest child

My children, show these same, entangled threads
Perhaps, they live their lives, like so many
too much in their heads
I would protect them, if I could, from all their dreads
…especially, that sweet youngest child

My life is a composite
I have been Maiden, Mother, and now Crone
Inner strength prevails, an overflowing heart
but now with weakened bone
Once I danced, my fluid skills I'd hone
and dance I will
the youngest child
…until I am called home

The Piper's Call

In the blink of an eye we're gone from here
to play in the breeze that blows away all fear
As the west wind howls and the piper calls
we follow in the dance, held in Her thrall
On we dance to the sound of music so sweet
Swept on in the rhythm of Her pulsing heart beat
Through the realms of night into brightest day
till we reach the Summer-country
on the Crooked Path's Way
Where our tears are dried and the pain is done
We dance on again laughing
for we're free, we've won
Though battle weary, we fear no harm
for the piper's trill calls us
…to the Mother's waiting arms

About the Author

Renowned clairvoyant and a teacher of the Western Mysteries at Daylesford School of Arcane Knowledge, Penny Reilly is an initiated Bard and Ovate in the Tradition of the Druid. Penny has a passion for the Old Ways of the British Isles; returning there this year to carry out research for her nonfiction books her second series 'Cloak of Magick' and a Cornish folklore volume, forthcoming.

She feels that the gentle path of the Druid is the path to take for a sustainable future, connecting us to the land, no matter where we live on the planet. She describes herself as a 'nature writer'. Her poetry, inspired by Nature, is her connection to her personal environment.

Her own visionary experiences are very much a part of her storyline, poetry and lyrics …this is her sixth published book. Her controversial series Silver's Threads is still gaining popularity and the poems herein are from this five-volume fantasy work.

Penny moved to Sydney, Australia in 1980 and to the central highlands of Victoria with her husband David, 20 years ago. They share space with an 'all sorts' terrier, an old tabby cat, a small flock of hens and a fat wombat fondly known as 'chocolat', who has adopted them.

Keen gardeners, they are becoming self-sufficient on their beautiful rolling acres on the Great Divide; their blended mob of children are long 'grown and flown' the coop. Together they own Daylesford Tarot Readers, 'earthly rites bookshop' and Beyond the Gate Gallery and Nursery, which features Penny's other passion, photography (included in this volume).

You can find out more about the author, her books, poetry, gallery, nursery, tours and workshops at…

http://www.silversthreads.com
http://www.amazon.com/pennyreilly
http://www.facebook.com/pennyreillyauthorpage
http://www.facebook.com/earthlyrites
http://www.goodreads.com/pennyreilly
Sales direct from http://daylesfordtarot.com

www.ingramcontent.com/pod-product-compliance
Lightning Source LLC
Chambersburg PA
CBHW050537300426
44113CB00012B/2155